WORLD ANIMALS

by Linda Sonntag

Silver Dolphin

San Diego, California

Silver Dolphin Books
An imprint of the Baker & Taylor Publishing Group
10350 Barnes Canyon Road, San Diego, CA 92121
www.silverdolphinbooks.com

Copyright ©2014 Studio Fun International, Inc.
44 South Broadway, White Plains, NY 10601 U.S.A. and
Studio Fun International Limited,
The Ice House, 124-126 Walcot Street, Bath UK BA1 5BG
All rights reserved.

Text copyright ©2014 Flowerpot Press
Designed by Flowerpot Press
Consultants: Richard Walker Ph.D. and Don Moore MPA, Ph.D.

"Silver Dolphin" is a registered trademark of Baker & Taylor.
All rights reserved.

ISBN-13: 978-1-62686-302-6
ISBN-10: 1-62686-302-4

First published in the United States in 2000 by Copper Beech Books, an imprint of
The Millbrook Press, 2 Old New Milford Road, Brookfield, Connecticut 06804

Manufactured, printed, and assembled in China.
1 2 3 4 5 18 17 16 15 14
HH1/07/14

CONTENTS

INTRODUCTION

Welcome to the wonderful world of animals!

Animals are found almost everywhere on the earth's surface—across the continents of North and South America, Europe, Asia, Africa, and Australia; in the polar regions of Antarctica and the Arctic; on remote islands and in the vast oceans.

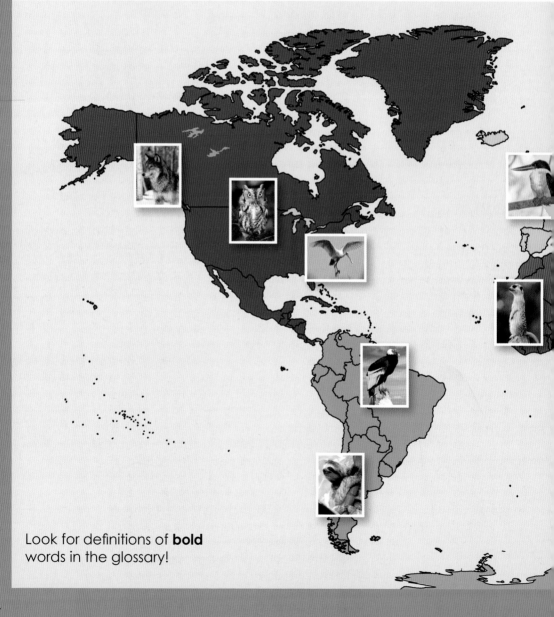

Look for definitions of **bold** words in the glossary!

They live high in the mountains and graze in meadows. They swim deep in the ocean and hop near ponds. They climb trees and slide on ice.

Where an animal lives can tell us a lot about the animal. We can learn how it finds food, where it sleeps, and how it moves from one place to another. This book will introduce you to all of the regions of the world and to many different **habitats.**

Along the way, you will meet many animals that will amaze you.

CLASSIFICATION

The animal kingdom is an amazing, diverse group of living things. It includes tiny insects and gigantic whales, swimming sharks and waddling penguins, gentle zebras and prowling lions.

To keep track of all the plants and animals in the world, scientists use a classification system. Living things with similar features, or traits, are grouped together. The largest group is called a kingdom. The smallest group is called a species.

To find out how the classification system works, let's look at how the lion is classified as a member of the animal kingdom.

You know that lions are big, furry animals that have backbones and eat meat, right? Well, that's because the lion is a member of the large cat genus and the cat family. All cats eat meat, so they are members of the carnivore order. They also have fur and give birth to live young, so they are part of the mammal class; mammals have backbones, so they are part of the vertebrate phylum.

Take a look at the chart on the next page to see the lion classification and other animals that share each group.

DID YOU KNOW?

Over two million animal species have been identified so far.

KINGDOM
Animals (Animalia)

Lion
Panthera leo

Macaw
Ara macao

Octopus
Octopus vulgaris

Blue morpho butterfly
Morpho retenor

Sponge
Clathria Sp.

PHYLUM
Vertebrates (Chordata)

Lion
Panthera leo

Harpy eagle
Harpia harpyja

Gila monster
Heloderma suspectum

Clownfish
Amphiprion percula

Tiger shark
Galeocerdo cuvieri

CLASS
Mammals (Mammalia)

Lion
Panthera leo

American beaver
Castor canadensis

Gorilla
Gorilla gorilla

Leopard seal
Hydrurga leptonyx

Red kangaroo
Macropus rufus

ORDER
Meat eaters (Carnivora)

Lion
Panthera leo

African wild dog
Lycaon pictus

Brown bear
Ursus arctos

Meerkat
Suricata suricatta

Pine marten
Martes martes

FAMILY
Cats (Felidae)

Lion
Panthera leo

Domestic cat
Felis catus

Cougar
Puma concolor

European wildcat
Felis silvestris

Jaguar
Panthera onca

GENUS
Large cats (Panthera)

Lion
Panthera leo

Tiger
Panthera tigris

Jaguar
Panthera onca

Leopard
Panthera pardus

SPECIES
Lion (Panthera leo)

Lion
Panthera leo

7

SOUTH AMERICA

South America has a unique set of animals, such as sloths, opossums, New World monkeys, and anteaters. South America also has the world's richest bird life. Nearly half the world's bird species spend some time here. The greatest **diversity** of animals lives near the mighty Amazon River. The lush, dense Amazon rain forest in the north of the continent is home to millions of species.

The Andes Mountains run down the west side of the continent, from Venezuela to Chile. Between the central section of the Andes and the Pacific is the hot Atacama Desert, one of the driest places on earth. In some areas, it has not rained for hundreds of years.

Grasslands, including the Pampas, fill much of the central and southern parts of South America.

Spectacled bear
The only bear native to South America, this bear lives in the Andes Mountains and is named for the circles around its eyes.

Capybara
Making its home near water in the Pampas region, the capybara is the size of a pig and is related to the guinea pig.

Poison dart frog
These brightly colored frogs can be red, green, blue, or black, and make their home in the Amazon. They are among the most poisonous animals on earth.

Gulf of Venezuela
L. Maracaibo
GUYANA
SURINAM
FRENCH GUIANA
VENEZUELA
Cauca R.
Meta R.
Orinoco R.
Guyana Highlands
Marajo Island
Malpelo
COLOMBIA
Branco R.
ATLANTIC OCEAN
f of aquil
ECUADOR
Putumayo R.
Negro R.
Amazon R.
Amazon R.
Amazon Basin
Parnaiba R.
Brazilian Highlands
Purus R.
Madeira R.
Tapajos R.
Xingu R.
Araguaia R.
Tocantins R.
Ucayali R.
PERU
B R A Z I L
São Francisco R.
A n d e s
L. Titicaca
BOLIVIA
Paraguay R.
Plateau of Mato Grosso
PACIFIC OCEAN
Atacama Desert
Gran Chaco
PARAGUAY
Parana R.
Salado R.
Parana R.
Uruguay R.
A n d e s
ARGENTINA
Pampas
URUGUAY
River Plate
C H I L E
Colorado R.
Negro R.
Valdes Peninsula
Chico R.
Gulf of San Jorge
Deseado R.
Falkland Islands (UK)

Tierra del Fuego
Cape Horn

0		Miles		1,000
0		Kilometers		1,600

9

ANDES

The world's longest mountain chain, the Andes, stretches over 4,500 miles down the western side of South America. The western slopes are dry, while the eastern side has more rain, vegetation, and animals. Many peaks are snow-covered. The lower slopes contain tropical forests, home to the spectacled bear, northern pudu, and the shy Andean tapir.

Andean condor
Like all vultures, the Andean condor has a bald head and neck. The world's largest bird of prey, it has a wingspan of 10½ feet.

■ Andes

DID YOU KNOW?

*The smallest member of the camel family, the vicuña, grazes the high meadows of the Andes. Recent **conservation** projects have saved the vicuña from extinction, and there are now about 85,000, found mostly in national parks.*

Andean flicker
This woodpecker searches under bark for insects and uses its long, sticky tongue to catch ants and other bugs.

Northern pudu
The smallest of the world's deer, the northern pudu is only 15 inches high. This secretive animal feeds on leaves, shoots, and fruit.

Hummingbird
There are more than 300 species of hummingbirds, and most live in Central and South America. These tiny birds got their name from the sound their speedy wings make.

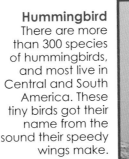

Mountain viscacha
This very agile animal looks like a long-tailed rabbit. It is a member of the rodent family.

Cougar
The cougar has many names, including puma, mountain lion, and panther. They live all along the Andes and are also found in North America. They can leap 20 feet into a tree and cover more than 33 feet over the ground in one bound.

AMAZON RAIN FOREST

The Amazon rain forest of South America is the world's largest rain forest, covering nearly 2.3 million square miles. It contains the greatest variety of animal life in the world and nearly half of all bird species—including 300 types of hummingbirds. The loud screeching of macaws fills the air, as do the booming calls of howler monkeys.

Bright colors are everywhere, from the wings of butterflies to the warning patterns on poisonous frogs. Their brightly colored skin warns predators, especially birds, that they are toxic! The rain forest is hot, **humid**, and wet all year round, which is ideal for the many species of trees, vines, and ferns.

■ Amazon rain forest

Jaguar
The jaguar hunts quietly at night, feeding on anything from mice to tapirs. An excellent swimmer, it catches fish by flipping them out of the water with its paw.

Piranha

Piranhas hunt by smell, and use their razor-sharp teeth to eat other fish, as well as worms and insects.

Macaw

The largest of the South American parrots, the scarlet macaw feeds on fruit and nuts, using its foot as a "hand" to hold its food. Its hooked beak is so strong that it is the only bird able to crack a Brazil nut!

Sloth

The three-toed sloth sleeps by day and eats leaves by night, hanging upside down in a tree by its long, hooked claws. It can turn its head 270 degrees, so it can see all around. The sloth is slow-moving and may live in the same tree for years.

DID YOU KNOW? ?

The destruction of the Amazon rain forest—for lumber, mining, and farmland—could wipe out half the world's animal species. At the current rate of destruction, no forest at all will be left by 2035.

Harpy eagle

The largest and most powerful eagle in the world is the harpy eagle. It can carry off creatures as large as monkeys and sloths in its huge, powerful **talons**, and also feeds on opossums and snakes.

NORTH AMERICA

North America stretches from the cold **polar** regions of northern Canada to the tropical forests of Central America in the south, and is bordered by the mighty Pacific Ocean in the west and the Atlantic in the east. North America has two mountain chains—the high Rockies run down the west side, while the Appalachians rise in the east. Stretched out between the two mountain chains are the fertile Great Plains, and forests cover much of the north.

Warm wetlands in the southeast form an ideal habitat for water birds and alligators. By contrast, the southwest is a dry area of deserts, where many animals seek shade during the day and emerge to feed at night.

DID YOU KNOW?

*The Virginia opossum, which lives in the eastern part of the United States and in Mexico, is North America's only **marsupial**. Like the kangaroo, it has a pouch on its belly to carry its young.*

Mountain bluebird
In the summer, the mountain bluebird lives high in the mountains of western North America, feeding on insects. In the winter, bluebirds move down the mountains and gather in flocks to feed on fruit.

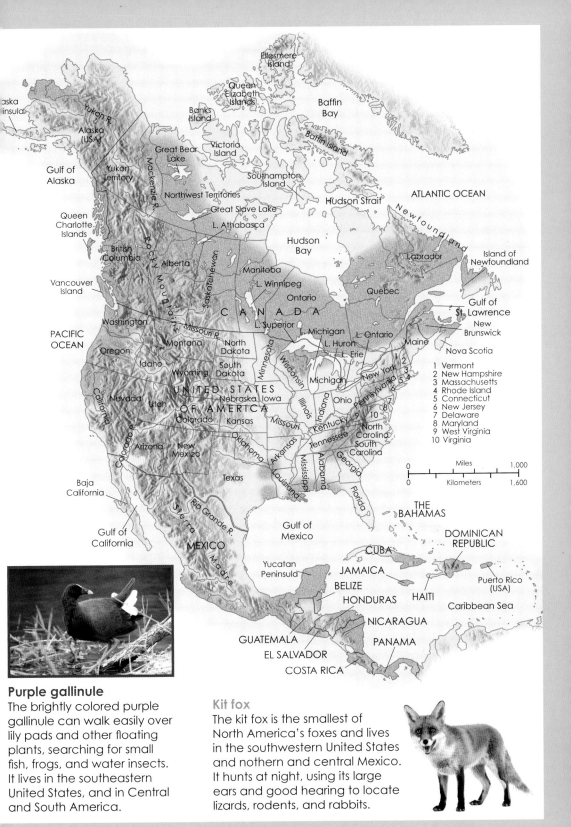

Ellesmere Island
Queen Elizabeth Islands
Banks Island
Baffin Bay
Aska insula
Yukon R.
Alaska (USA)
Great Bear Lake
Victoria Island
Baffin Island
Gulf of Alaska
Yukon Territory
Mackenzie R.
Southampton Island
Northwest Territories
ATLANTIC OCEAN
Queen Charlotte Islands
Great Slave Lake
Hudson Strait
Newfoundland
L. Athabasca
British Columbia
Rocky Mountains
Alberta
Saskatchewan
Manitoba
Hudson Bay
Labrador
Island of Newfoundland
Vancouver Island
L. Winnipeg
Ontario
Quebec
Gulf of St. Lawrence
PACIFIC OCEAN
Washington
Montana
North Dakota
L. Superior
L. Michigan
L. Huron
L. Ontario
L. Erie
New Brunswick
Maine
Nova Scotia
Oregon
Idaho
Missouri R.
Minnesota
Wisconsin
Michigan
New York
C A N A D A
U N I T E D   S T A T E S
O F   A M E R I C A
California
Nevada
Utah
Wyoming
South Dakota
Nebraska
Iowa
Illinois
Indiana
Ohio
Pennsylvania
Colorado
Colorado R.
Kansas
Missouri
Kentucky
West Virginia
North Carolina
South Carolina
Arizona
New Mexico
Oklahoma
Arkansas
Tennessee
Alabama
Georgia
Baja California
Texas
Sierra Madre
Rio Grande R.
Mississippi
Louisiana
Florida
Gulf of California
MEXICO
Gulf of Mexico
THE BAHAMAS
Yucatan Peninsula
CUBA
JAMAICA
BELIZE
HONDURAS
HAITI
DOMINICAN REPUBLIC
Puerto Rico (USA)
Caribbean Sea
GUATEMALA
EL SALVADOR
COSTA RICA
NICARAGUA
PANAMA

1 Vermont
2 New Hampshire
3 Massachusetts
4 Rhode Island
5 Connecticut
6 New Jersey
7 Delaware
8 Maryland
9 West Virginia
10 Virginia

Miles
0   1,000
0   1,600
Kilometers

Purple gallinule
The brightly colored purple gallinule can walk easily over lily pads and other floating plants, searching for small fish, frogs, and water insects. It lives in the southeastern United States, and in Central and South America.

Kit fox
The kit fox is the smallest of North America's foxes and lives in the southwestern United States and nothern and central Mexico. It hunts at night, using its large ears and good hearing to locate lizards, rodents, and rabbits.

FLORIDA EVERGLADES

The subtropical Everglades is the world's largest wetland. It is largely **marshland**, dotted with ponds and islands of trees. The Everglades (mostly contained within a national park) covers about 2,300 square miles of the southern tip of the Florida peninsula. The shallow, fish-filled ponds are called "gator holes" because they are widened and deepened by American alligators. They attract fish-eating water birds, such as herons and spoonbills.

Everglades

The richness of animal life in the Everglades depends on the flooding that takes place after the dry winter months. In the north, heavy rains cause Lake Okeechobee to overflow, and this forms a river, which covers the Everglades. As the runoff spreads, water levels rise and river animals move freely throughout the park.

American alligator
The American alligator digs out the swamp to keep it flooded and well stocked with prey (freshwater turtles, fish, and snakes).

Roseate spoonbill
Like flamingoes, the roseate spoonbill has pink legs and feathers because of the pink pigment in the shrimp it eats. They sweep their bills from side to side in the water, snapping up food by touch.

Everglade kite
The Everglade kite is also called the "snail kite" because it feeds most exclusively on a type of water snail (the apple snail).

Cottonmouth
The cottonmouth snake is aggressive and dangerous. Also called the "water moccasin," it eats fish, frogs, salamanders, other snakes, birds, and small mammals.

Anhinga
The anhinga swims underwater with its neck above the water. It could be mistaken for a swimming snake, which is why it is also called the "snakebird."

DID YOU KNOW? ?

For nine months of the year, floodwaters fill the swamps and marshlands of the Everglades. But in the 1980s, a drainage program was started to take water from Lake Okeechobee for use in cities, and to irrigate farmland. Low water levels are now threatening the Everglades. Named a World Heritage Site in 1979, the Everglades is dependent on conservation efforts for its survival.

WESTERN DESERTS

North America's desert regions extend from northern Mexico into the southwestern United States. When it rains, the water rapidly **evaporates** into the ground. Death Valley, which is one of the hottest places on earth, with temperatures of up to 129°F, is part of the western deserts. Most desert animals seek shelter during the day in **burrows** or under stones, cacti, or other plants, and come out at night to feed, when it is cooler.

Western deserts

Death Valley

Desert tortoise
The shell of the desert tortoise protects the animal from the scorching sun. If threatened, the tortoise draws its head and legs back into its shell until the danger has passed.

Gila monster
The black-and-yellow pattern on this large lizard warns other aimals to stay away. It is one of only two types of lizards with a poisonous bite.

Black-tailed jackrabbit
This animal's enormous ears give it great hearing and act as a radiator to release heat. Jackrabbits rarely drink water—they get moisture from nibbling on cactus leaves.

Roadrunner
This bird can fly, but prefers to run—and it can run fast! Reaching speeds of 19 miles per hour, it can outrun most of its predators.

DID YOU KNOW?

The western diamondback rattlesnake's eyes let in lots of light for good vision. It also has pit **organs**— heat-sensitive **membranes** between its eyes and nostrils—to help "see" prey. It flicks out its forked tongue to taste the air for scents of its prey.

PRAIRIES

The word "prairie" comes from the French for "large meadow," but the North American prairies are more than large meadows. They are also bitterly cold in the winter and hot in the summer. Today, widespread **agriculture** has left few areas of natural prairie. The prairie soil, among the richest in the world, is used to grow wheat, corn, and other grains. Other areas are grazed by cattle and sheep, which has pushed out the native prairie species.

Prairie

Prairies

Burrowing owl
The burrowing owl makes its home underground. It can dig with its feet and beak, but prefers to move into an abandoned prairie dog hole.

Coyote
Distinguished by its mournful howl, the coyote is a relative of the wolf. It lives alone and hunts at dusk for jackrabbits, prairie dogs, and other rodents.

Prairie dog

The prairie dog is a type of burrowing squirrel. A network of tunnels connect the huge underground home for thousands of animals.

Sage grouse

The male sage grouse puffs out his breast, inflates air sacs in his neck, and makes popping calls. It gets its name from the sagebrush plant, on which it feeds.

DID YOU KNOW?

The striped skunk is a night hunter that feeds on insects and small mammals. It spends most of the time by itself. When threatened, the skunk turns its back on its enemy, raising its bushy tail, scratching with its front feet, and hissing loudly. If the enemy does not retreat, the skunk then sprays a stinking, stinging fluid from a gland in its bottom.

Bison

Great herds of bison once grazed their way across the prairies. When their numbers were threatened, bison were given protected status in national parks. Bison can live to be 40 years old.

Long-nosed armadillo

The horny plates of the common long-nosed armadillo protect it from predators. If attacked, it lies flat with its legs tucked in, or rolls into a ball.

FORESTS AND WOODLANDS

NORTH AMERICA

Coniferous forests of spruce, pine, larch, and fir stretch for almost 4,000 miles, from Alaska and across most of Canada. Here, the summers are warm, but the winters are bitterly cold. The lynx and its main prey, the snowshoe hare, have thickly furred feet to keep them from sinking into deep snow. The short summer brings insect-eating birds, and the caribou (reindeer) leave for the colder north. Birds of prey feed on rodents that are plentiful in the summer.

The woodlands are filled with over 150 species of **deciduous**, broad-leaved trees, including maple, oak, and beech. These provide a rich habitat for many animals—rodents, birds, raccoons, and opossums to name a few.

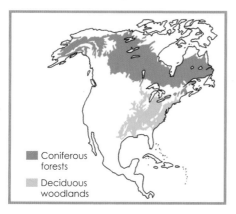

Coniferous forests

Deciduous woodlands

Fall in a North American forest

Moose
In the winter, moose feed on trees and bushes in forests across the far north of the continent. In the summer, their main diet is water plants—they often wade up to their shoulders in marshy lakes to feed. Moose need about 45 pounds of vegetation a day to keep them going.

Spring peeper

The spring peeper is a tree frog less than an inch long. Sticky pads on its long, thin fingers and toes give a good grip while it climbs trees in search of insect prey.

Woodpecker

A rapid drumming noise often signals the presence of a red-headed woodpecker. The spongy bone at the base of the woodpecker's beak acts as a cushion against the hammering.

Porcupine

Long toe claws and an excellent sense of balance help the North American porcupine climb trees in search of new shoots and fruit. If attacked, it raises its spines and lashes its barbed tail from side to side.

Beaver

With their huge incisor teeth, beavers cut down trees, which they nudge and float into position across fast-flowing streams. Then they build dams with sticks, stones, and mud, creating a large pool.

DID YOU KNOW?

The eastern screech owl roosts in a hole in a tree and hunts at night for insects, birds, and squirrels. Owls have great hearing and large, light-sensitive eyes. They fly silently with down-covered flight feathers that muffle the air passing through them.

EUROPE

Europe is the second smallest continent after Australia. Attracted by the mild climate and rich, fertile soils, Europe's dense human population has greatly reduced the number of animals. Some wolves and bears remain in what's left of the forests. In the far north, winters are very cold, so animals such as pine martens and wolves live there.

Europe's mountains, the largest of which are the Alps and the Pyrenees, provide a natural barrier that protects the south from rain and cold winds. Southern Europe has a warm, dry climate with a range of animals, including frogs, fish, lizards, tortoises, and water birds.

Wolf
The European wolf travels in small packs that hunt together for livestock. Though they were almost **extinct** at one point, they are now growing at a steady rate, with the largest populations now in eastern Europe.

Otter
The Eurasian otter lives by riverbanks and the seashore throughout Europe, and eats shellfish and fish. Its ears and nostrils close when it dives, and its streamlined body allows it to move quickly through the water.

Wildcat
The wildcat was once found all over Europe, but is now rare, living primarily in the forests and grasslands. European wildcats live alone, and females make their nests in hollow trees.

Jay
The Eurasian jay lives secretively in its woodland habitat. In the fall, it buries a winter food store of acorns in the ground—usually one in each spot—and remembers where to find most of them months later.

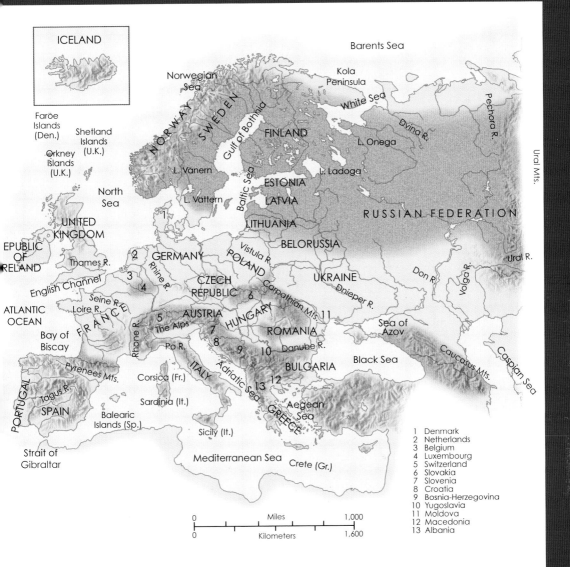

ICELAND

Faröe
Islands
(Den.)

Shetland
Islands
(U.K.)

Orkney
Islands
(U.K.)

North
Sea

Barents Sea

Kola
Peninsula

Norwegian
Sea

NORWAY

SWEDEN

Gulf of Bothnia

White Sea

L. Onega

Dvina R.

Pechora R.

Ural Mts.

FINLAND

L. Ladoga

L. Vänern

Baltic Sea

L. Vattern

ESTONIA

LATVIA

RUSSIAN FEDERATION

Ural R.

UNITED
KINGDOM

EPUBLIC
OF
RELAND

Thames R.

1

LITHUANIA

BELORUSSIA

Vistula R.

2 GERMANY

POLAND

CZECH
REPUBLIC

UKRAINE

Dnieper R.

Don R.

Volga R.

English Channel

Rhine R.

3
4

6

Carpathian Mts.

11

Sea of
Azov

Caucasus Mts.

Caspian Sea

Seine R.

ATLANTIC
OCEAN

Loire R.

FRANCE

Rhone R.

5 AUSTRIA

The Alps

7

HUNGARY

ROMANIA

Bay of
Biscay

Po R.

8

Danube R.

Black Sea

Pyrenees Mts.

Corsica (Fr.)

ITALY

9

10

BULGARIA

PORTUGAL

Tagus R.

SPAIN

Sardinia (It.)

Adriatic Sea

13 12

Aegean
Sea

Balearic
Islands (Sp.)

Sicily (It.)

GREECE

Strait of
Gibraltar

Mediterranean Sea

Crete (Gr.)

1 Denmark
2 Netherlands
3 Belgium
4 Luxembourg
5 Switzerland
6 Slovakia
7 Slovenia
8 Croatia
9 Bosnia-Herzegovina
10 Yugoslavia
11 Moldova
12 Macedonia
13 Albania

Miles	1,000
0	
0	1,600
Kilometers	

Brown bear
The brown bear lives in the
mountains of southern Europe.
Its diet includes berries, nuts,
roots, fish (such as salmon),
and rodents. The females sleep
through the cold months, when
food is scarce, and emerge in
the spring with their cubs!

FORESTS

EUROPE

In the fall, trees lose their leaves as they prepare for the winter. In the spring, there is a rebirth. Buds burst open and new leaves and flowers appear, turning the forests green. Insects hatch out to feed on the young leaves and suck sap from stems. In turn, they provide food for birds, such as treecreepers, that have arrived in the woods to lay their eggs in nests high in the branches. Deer feed on grasses and flowers that appear in clearings, and squirrels scramble up and down tree trunks as they **forage** for seeds and fruits, while foxes hunt for small prey such as mice. Fallen leaves on the forest floor are home to many insects, and nourish the soil.

During the summer months, young animals grow and become independent. By the fall, as the trees shed their leaves again, the forests provide a feast of fruits, nuts, and fungi.

Stag beetles
Male stag beetles have huge, antler-shaped jaws, which they wave to attract females.

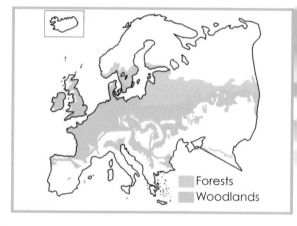

Forests
Woodlands

Hedgehog
The European hedgehog is covered in as many as 5,000 sharp spines. If threatened, it raises its spines by tensing muscles under the skin. If danger persists, it rolls itself into a spiny ball.

Cutting down trees to make room to grow crops destroys the homes of wild birds that feed on insect pests. **Pesticides** are sprayed to control these insects. Unfortunately, the pesticides also kill many useful insects, such as bees and ladybugs.

Eurasian sparrowhawk

The sparrowhawk flies close to the ground, looking for prey (mainly other birds), which it catches after a short, fast chase. The female sparrowhawk is larger than the male.

Eurasian badger

Badgers are **omnivores**, eating both small animals and plants. They have poor eyesight and rely on their sense of smell to find food at night. Badgers weigh between 15 and 29 pounds in the spring, but bulk up to 33 to 37 pounds in the fall to get ready for hibernating in the winter.

European mole

Moles live underground in a system of tunnels. Their main diet is earthworms that fall into the tunnels. Moles have poorly developed senses of smell, sight, and hearing, but can sense small vibrations in the soil, such as other moles banging their heads against the walls of their tunnels to warn neighbors about predators.

WETLANDS

EUROPE

Europe's wetlands are home to an endless variety of creatures suited to life in or near water. Waterside plants provide shelter for many of these animals. Wetlands provide important feeding and breeding grounds for many bird species, and are a stopping point for birds migrating across Europe. In the summer, wetlands are alive with insects. Insects are eaten by frogs and newts. Both these amphibians—as well as fish—are prey to birds such as herons, diving mammals like otters and water shrews, and large, sharp-toothed fish such as pike.

In many parts of Europe, wetland wildlife is threatened because of the pollution of water by fertilizers, the pesticides from farmland, and poisonous waste from factories. Western Europe has now lost most of its natural wetlands; those that remain, although protected, are still at risk.

Pike
The pike is an excellent hunter. It waits motionless in weeds, then shoots out and grabs its prey.

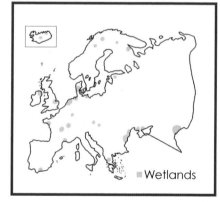

■Wetlands

European wetland

In the spring, male frogs gather in ponds and croak to attract females. Frog eggs hatch into tadpoles, which have gills like fish. The tadpoles develop arms and legs, lose their tails, and their gills become lungs.

Water shrew
The water shrew needs a constant supply of food to keep it warm, so it eats and sleeps in short bursts all day and night.

Heron
The heron wades through water, then waits motionless for a fish to swim by, or it slowly stalks its prey on the riverbank. Then it strikes quickly, grabbing its victim with its long, pointed beak.

Kingfisher
The kingfisher lives by shallow waters with lots of small fish. It dives into the water, grabs its prey, hits it against a branch to stun it, and eats it whole.

AFRICA

Africa is the world's second largest continent. In northern Africa is the Sahara Desert, which covers 3.5 million square miles—an area as big as the United States.

Tropical rain forest stretches from the Gulf of Guinea in the west across the Congo Basin. The hot, wet environment is home to the tiny royal antelope, the enormous Goliath beetle, and richly colored birds such as the Congo peafowl. The rain forest gives way to savanna— vast expanses of open grassland, home to the world's largest herds of grazing animals, as well as the big cats, scavenging dogs, and vultures.

East Africa is dominated by the Great Rift Valley—huge cracks in the earth's crust that have flooded in places to form a chain of long, deep lakes. Crocodiles lurk in the shallows, flocks of pink flamingoes feed on tiny shrimp, eagles soar over mountain ranges, baboons and ibex leap across crags, and hippos wallow in the water.

Impala
The impala is a grass eater that **migrates** in herds across the savanna. In the early summer, the females each have a single calf. The young are watched over by their mothers until they are strong enough to run with the herd.

Gorilla
Gorillas are the world's largest apes. They live in family groups in the forests of central Africa and feed on leaves, shoots, and stems. A mature male, known as a silverback because of the color of his hair, leads the group. Females and their young climb into trees to feed and sleep. If challenged by a young male, a silverback will roar and beat his chest.

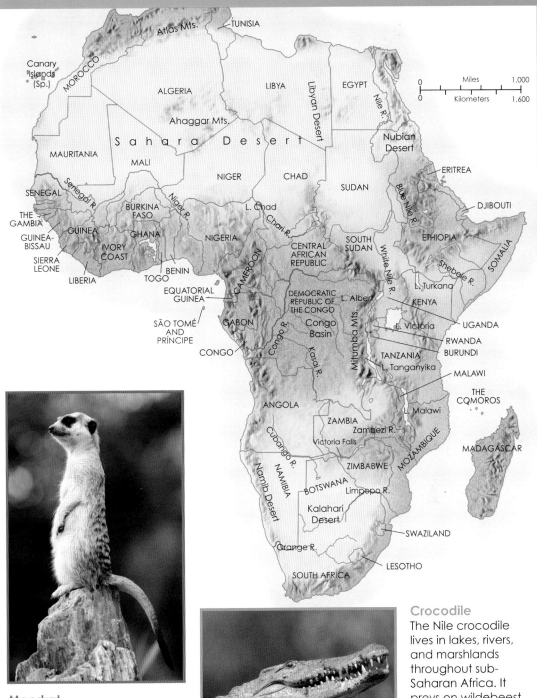

TUNISIA
Atlas Mts.
Canary Islands (Sp.)
MOROCCO
ALGERIA
LIBYA
Libyan Desert
EGYPT
Nile R.
Ahaggar Mts.
Sahara Desert
Nubian Desert
MAURITANIA
MALI
NIGER
CHAD
SUDAN
ERITREA
Senegal R.
SENEGAL
BURKINA FASO
Niger R.
L. Chad
Chari R.
Blue Nile R.
DJIBOUTI
THE GAMBIA
GUINEA-BISSAU
GUINEA
GHANA
NIGERIA
CENTRAL AFRICAN REPUBLIC
SOUTH SUDAN
ETHIOPIA
SOMALIA
SIERRA LEONE
IVORY COAST
BENIN
TOGO
White Nile R.
Shebele R.
LIBERIA
EQUATORIAL GUINEA
CAMEROON
DEMOCRATIC REPUBLIC OF THE CONGO
L. Albert
L. Turkana
KENYA
SÃO TOMÉ AND PRÍNCIPE
GABON
Congo R.
Congo Basin
Mitumba Mts.
L. Victoria
UGANDA
CONGO
Kasai R.
TANZANIA
L. Tanganyika
RWANDA
BURUNDI
MALAWI
ANGOLA
L. Malawi
THE COMOROS
ZAMBIA
Zambezi R.
Cubango R.
Victoria Falls
MOZAMBIQUE
MADAGASCAR
Namib Desert
NAMIBIA
ZIMBABWE
BOTSWANA
Limpopo R.
Kalahari Desert
SWAZILAND
Orange R.
LESOTHO
SOUTH AFRICA

Miles 0 1,000
Kilometers 0 1,600

Meerkat
The meerkat is a rabbit-sized animal that lives in the deserts and dry areas of southern Africa. These sociable relatives of the mongoose live in groups and share the work.

Crocodile
The Nile crocodile lives in lakes, rivers, and marshlands throughout sub-Saharan Africa. It preys on wildebeest, gazelle, buffalo, and lions. The crocodile ambushes its prey, then drags it underwater to drown it.

SAVANNA

The African savanna is one of the last great natural grasslands on earth. It is home to many of the world's largest land mammals, both grazing animals and their predators. Zebras and gazelle eat grasses, and elephants and giraffes eat leaves from tall trees. Lions, leopards, wild dogs, and vultures feed on these herbivores.

Though the savanna is warm year-round, it has two very different seasons: a wet season (summer) when it rains every afternoon for hours, and a dry season (winter), in which no rain falls at all. Both seasons are very hot. As the grasses become parched, the herds move to fresh grazing lands. When the warm rains come, the land turns green.

Savanna

Rhino
Rhinos can weigh as much as two tons. Though they are big, stocky animals, rhinos can run up to 30 miles per hour!

Zebras
For most of the year, zebras live in scattered groups of 10 to 15 animals, usually one male and the rest females and their foals. In the dry season, they merge into big groups, to find safety in numbers.

Ostrich

The world's largest bird, the ostrich, cannot fly, but it can run faster than any other animal on two legs, sprinting up to 43 miles per hour! An ostrich egg is 20 times bigger than a hen's egg.

Wildebeest

These grazing, horned animals are active both day and night. Herds of wildebeest and zebra often join together to provide greater protection against predators, such as lions.

African dog

This wild dog lives in packs of up to 20 individuals. They are very social animals, sharing care for the young, old, and sick in the pack.

Secretary bird

With wings that span 6½ feet, these giant birds can soar like other birds of prey, but spend much of their time walking on land. They feed on rodents, insects, and snakes.

DID YOU KNOW?

Lions live in a pride of 20 to 30 animals. Each pride has up to four males, distinguished by their manes. Male cubs leave the pride at two years old. The lionesses do most of the work, sharing cub care and hunting in an organized group while the males rest.

DESERTS

The Sahara is the largest desert on earth. The scorching sun beats down by day, but at night it gets extremely cold, and hardly ever rains. The creatures that live in the Sahara and Africa's southern deserts, the Kalahari and the Namib Deserts, have adapted to survive harsh conditions. Insects, scorpions, and spiders have a hard, shiny skin to keep their bodies from drying out. Reptiles such as snakes and lizards need the sun's warmth to make them active. Some animals, like the sand cat, have thick fur under their feet to protect them from the hot ground.

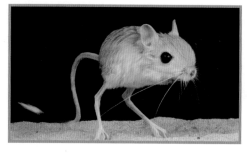

Jerboa
The desert jerboa is a small rodent that looks like a tiny kangaroo. Its strong back legs are four times as long as its front legs, and it can jump more than 8 feet to escape from predators.

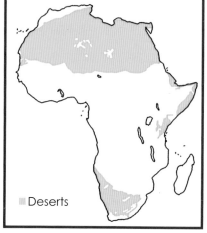

Deserts

Fennec fox
The fennec fox is the smallest of the foxes. Its huge ears, up to 6 inches long, help it keep cool in the Sahara heat.

Desert horned viper
The desert horned viper moves across the loose sand in an unusual way, leaving telltale "ladder" tracks. It burrows into the sand, leaving only its eyes and nostrils peeping out to watch for prey or danger.

The dromedary, or Arabian camel, has a single hump. This is made up mainly of fat, to keep the camel going. The camel can survive for weeks without food or drink, but when it gets to water, it will gulp nearly 14 gallons in a few minutes. In sandstorms, its long, thick eyelashes protect its eyes, and it can close its nostrils. Camels can travel up to 30 miles a day.

Addax
The addax can survive extreme heat and **drought**. It gets all its moisture from grasses and leaves and never needs to drink. Its wide hooves stop it from sinking into the sand as it searches for the scant desert vegetation.

Dabb spiny lizard
Reptiles control their body temperature by gaining or losing heat from the environment. The dabb spiny lizard can live on the fat stores in its tail if it can't find food, and also uses the spine on its tail for protection.

African sand dunes

ASIA

Asia is the largest continent in the world. While much of Asia consists of rolling plains, a central highland region called the Himalayas stretches from west to east. The highest point in these mountains is over 29,000 feet.

In the far north, coniferous forests known as the **taiga** have long, bitterly cold winters and are home only to animals that can survive the harsh conditions, like wolves and pine martens.

Farther south, the taiga gives way to **steppe** and then desert. The Himalayas separate these wastelands from India and tropical forests in Southeast Asia. The rapid increase in human population presents a serious threat to many Asian species. The tiger is the largest of the cat species, and was once widespread throughout Asia, but has been reduced to small, isolated populations and may become extinct in the wild.

Colugo
The colugo, a mammal known as the "flying lemur," has extra membranes on its arms that help it control its movements when it leaps from tree to tree in Southeast Asia.

Marbled polecat
The marbled polecat is found all over the steppe and semidesert. Although it is a good climber, the marbled polecat hunts mainly on the ground, leaving its burrow at dusk to hunt rodents, rabbits, frogs, lizards, snakes, and birds.

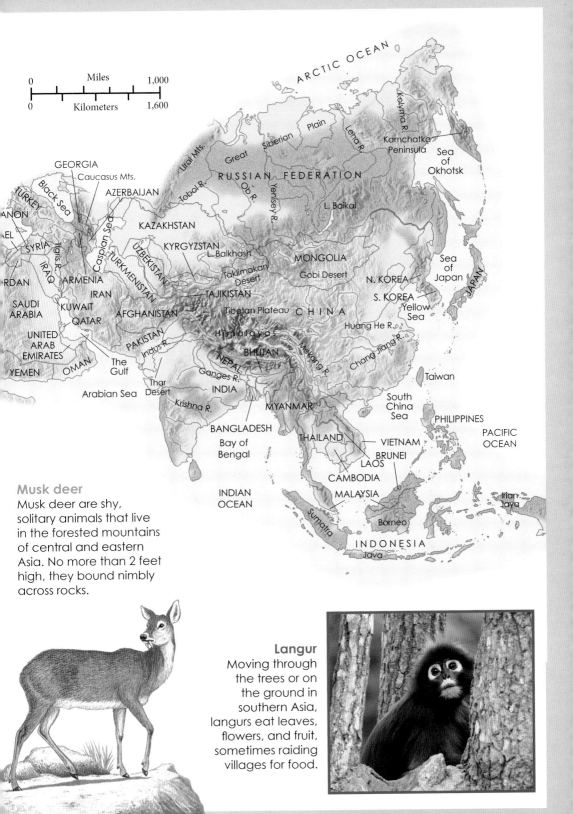

Miles
0   1,000

Kilometers
0   1,600

ARCTIC OCEAN

Kolyma R.

Plain
Siberian

Great
Plain

Lena R.

Kamchatka
Peninsula

Sea
of
Okhotsk

Ural Mts.

RUSSIAN FEDERATION

GEORGIA
Caucasus Mts.

AZERBAIJAN

Black Sea

TURKEY

Tobol R.

Ob' R.

Yenisey R.

L. Baikal

KAZAKHSTAN

ANON

SYRIA

Caspian Sea

KYRGYZSTAN

L. Balkhash

MONGOLIA

Sea
of
Japan

JAPAN

Tigris R.

IRAQ

ARMENIA

TURKMENISTAN

UZBEKISTAN

Taklimakan
Desert

Gobi Desert

N. KOREA

EL

RDAN

IRAN

TAJIKISTAN

Tibetan Plateau

CHINA

S. KOREA

Yellow
Sea

SAUDI
ARABIA

KUWAIT

QATAR

AFGHANISTAN

Huang He R.

KUWAIT

UNITED
ARAB
EMIRATES

PAKISTAN

Indus R.

Himalayas

NEPAL

BHUTAN

Mekong R.

Chang Jiang R.

Taiwan

YEMEN

OMAN

The
Gulf

Thar
Desert

Ganges R.

INDIA

Krishna R.

MYANMAR

South
China
Sea

PHILIPPINES

Arabian Sea

BANGLADESH

Bay of
Bengal

THAILAND

VIETNAM

PACIFIC
OCEAN

BRUNEI

LAOS

INDIAN
OCEAN

CAMBODIA

MALAYSIA

Sumatra

Borneo

Irian
Jaya

INDONESIA

Java

Musk deer

Musk deer are shy, solitary animals that live in the forested mountains of central and eastern Asia. No more than 2 feet high, they bound nimbly across rocks.

Langur

Moving through the trees or on the ground in southern Asia, langurs eat leaves, flowers, and fruit, sometimes raiding villages for food.

HIMALAYAS AND CHINA

The Himalayas form the great mountain system of Asia that separates the cold north from the tropical south. The vast ranges extend over 1,500 miles, from Pakistan across northern India to Bhutan, and include the highest peaks in the world, such as Mount Everest at 29,029 feet. While much of Asia is dry, parts of the Himalayas receive the world's highest rainfall.

On the snowcapped peaks, it is bitterly cold and nothing can survive. But the valleys at lower **altitudes** provide a mix of habitats for a wide range of animals. In the foothills, tropical forests teem with insects, frogs, lizards, snakes, birds, and mammals. Higher up, the tropical trees give way to forests of rhododendrons and bamboo.

Giant panda
Giant pandas live alone in the mountainous bamboo forests of southwestern China. Bamboo is so low in nutrients that giant pandas need to eat for 16 hours a day to get the food they need.

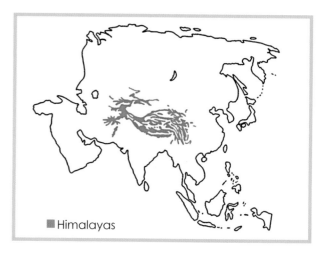

■ Himalayas

Golden pheasant
The male golden pheasant uses his colorful plumage to attract a female during the mating season. Golden pheasants build their nests on the ground in the forests of central China.

Snow leopard

The snow leopard lives high in the Himalayas. It preys on sheep, goats, and deer in the summer. In the winter, it follows its prey down to the valleys, where it finds gazelle and wild boar. The hairy pads under its paws help it leap across the snow without sinking.

Markhor

The markhor is a Himalayan goat with corkscrew horns that grow up to 4 feet on the male, and slightly shorter on the female. Hunters have brought the markhor to the edge of extinction.

DID YOU KNOW?

The chattering of the hill mynah can be heard in the tropical forests and plantations of the Himalayas and southern China. When tamed as pets, they can mimic almost any sound they hear.

Yak

Yaks are cattle that live on the high Tibetan plain. Their long, shaggy coats protect them from the cold, and they are surefooted enough to cope with the rough terrain. They provide humans with milk, meat, hides, and wool, and are used as pack animals and to pull carts.

TAIGA, STEPPE, AND DESERT

ASIA

The coniferous forest that forms the taiga of northern Asia is the largest forest in the world. The winters are long and harsh, but the short, warm summers see an explosion of life. The trees provide a rich source of food. Birds feed on the seeds of larch, spruce, and fir trees, as well as on the many insects. Birds of prey, like the goshawk, hunt these smaller birds. In the fall, most birds leave for warmer areas, while many mammals **hibernate**. To the south, the steppes have cold winters and hot, dry summers. The bison and antelope that used to live there have mostly disappeared.

The central Asian deserts lie south of the steppes. Summer days are hot, but temperatures plummet at night, and the winters are often icy cold. Here, animals, such as the Bactrian camel, have to withstand not only drought, but also extreme cold.

Onager
This member of the horse family can survive the harsh desert climate for two or three days without drinking.

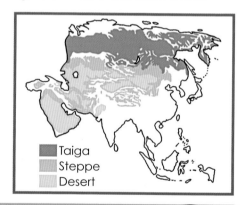

Taiga
Steppe
Desert

DID YOU KNOW?

The gray wolf can go for weeks without food, then eat up to 22 pounds of meat in one meal. Hunting in a pack, gray wolves concentrate on isolating one animal from the group and dragging it down. A kill can feed the pack for several days.

Pine marten

The large paws and sharp claws on the pine marten help it grip branches as it climbs trees. It also uses its long, bushy tail for balancing.

Suslik

These small animals live in colonies of thousands. They hibernate in burrows and their droppings fertilize the soil, helping new plants to grow.

Mongolian gerbil

During the day, this gerbil seeks shelter in its burrow, and is most active just before sunset. It is able to survive in the desert because it never needs to drink and doesn't sweat.

Great bustard

The male great bustard puts on an extraordinary display to attract a mate. He gulps in air to inflate a sac in his throat, which balloons out until his head is thrust back and he seems to turn inside out in a flurry of white feathers.

Baikal seal

Lake Baikal in Russia is the oldest and deepest lake in the world, and three-quarters of its animals are not found anywhere else on earth. The Baikal seal, the only seal found in fresh water, probably first arrived in the lake when the glaciers melted at the end of the last Ice Age, about 10,000 years ago.

AUSTRALASIA

Australasia includes Australia, New Zealand, and the surrounding islands, as well as Papua New Guinea (the eastern half of the island of New Guinea). Lying between the Indian and Pacific Oceans, Australia is the world's smallest continent. Since it's isolated, there are many unique animals, including the world's greatest variety of marsupial, or pouched, mammals, such as kangaroos and koalas.

Australia is mostly hot, dry desert, grassland, and **scrub**, known as the Outback. To the east of the Great Dividing Range, the climate is milder, with hot summers and cooler winters. New Guinea and northeastern Australia have tropical forests. A rich variety of animals live here, like the cuscus and tree kangaroo.

New Zealand has a warm, wet climate with few native mammals, including two types of bats and some swimming mammals. There are no native snakes to New Zealand and only one type of poisonous spider.

Spotted cuscus
The spotted cuscus is a tree-living marsupial from the rain forests of New Guinea and the Australian north. An excellent climber, the cuscus clings to branches with its feet and tail.

Brown falcon
The brown falcon hunts by watching motionless from a high perch, then swooping down on its prey in drier regions of Australia.

Koala
Koalas are marsupials that live in Australia. Koalas sleep more than 20 hours a day and carry their babies in their pouches.

New Ireland

Bougainville

Bismarck Sea

Central Range

PAPUA

NEW GUINEA

New Britain

SOLOMON ISLANDS

Choiseul

New Georgia

INDIAN OCEAN

Arafura Sea

Torres Strait

Cape York

Coral Sea

Timor Sea

Arnhem Land

Gulf of Carpentaria

Kimberley Plateau

Northern Territory

Fitzroy R.

Great Sandy Desert

A U S T R A L I A

Queensland

Great Dividing Range

Great Barrier Reef

Fraser Island

Gibson Desert

Macdonnell Ranges

Simpson Desert

Western Australia

Great Victoria Desert

L. Eyre

South Australia

New South Wales

Australian Alps

Darling R.

Great Australian Bight

Kangaroo Island

Murray R.

Victoria

Miles		1,000
0		
Kilometers		1,600
0		

Bass Strait

Tasman Sea

T a s m a n i a

Kangaroo
Kangaroos are large marsupials native to Australia and New Guinea. They can hop quickly on two legs or walk slowly on all four.

Tasman Sea

North Cape

North Island

East Cape

NEW ZEALAND

South Island

Southern Alps

SOUTH PACIFIC OCEAN

GREAT BARRIER REEF

The Great Barrier Reef is the largest coral reef in the world, and can be seen from outer space! It extends for 1,250 miles, off Australia's northeastern coast. Reefs grow in shallow tropical seas. Reefs are made of tiny skeletons of animals known as polyps. It takes hundreds of years for a reef to form.

The Great Barrier Reef contains over 400 species of coral. Around 1,500 species of fish live here. The moray eel lies in wait for prey in coral crevices; other fish swim in large schools, feeding on **plankton** and **algae**. Sharks patrol the reef, waiting for a fish to move away from its shelter. The reef also has over 4,000 species of mollusks, including sea slugs and octopuses that lurk in crevices before grabbing prey with their tentacles. Sea urchins, turtles, and sea cucumbers are also common.

Giant clam
This is one of the world's largest invertebrates, at 880 pounds and over 3 feet long. Its shell opens to feed, and shuts quickly when danger approaches.

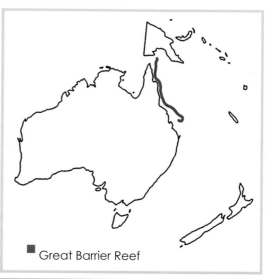

■ Great Barrier Reef

Olive sea snake
The flattened tail of the olive sea snake acts like a powerful paddle to thrust it through the water after its prey. Their venom stings their prey, which they then eat whole.

Clownfish

The clownfish hides among anemone that sting its predators. It also chases away butterfly fish, which feed on the anemone.

Brain coral

Corals are the hollow skeletons of thousands of polyps. This coral got its name because it looks like a human brain.

Blue-streaked cleaner wrasse

This tiny fish removes parasites from other fish. Even predators like the moray eel allow the wrasse to clean their teeth without harming it.

Tiger shark

The tiger shark swims off the reef as it searches for prey. Worn-out teeth are continuously replaced by rows of newer ones. The shark may use as many as 30,000 teeth in a lifetime!

DID YOU KNOW?

A coral reef is a fragile habitat and its complex food chain is easily disturbed. Reefs are threatened by overfishing and by souvenir hunters, boats, and pollution. Coral reefs can take hundreds of years to recover from damage.

Tubular sponge

Tubular sponges live on parts of the reef where there is plenty of food for them. They draw in water and filter out the nutrients. Many small creatures thrive in and around these sponges.

ANTARCTICA

Antarctica is the windiest, coldest, driest, and most isolated continent on earth. During the long, dark winter, temperatures can drop to -128°F, and the wind can gust at 125 miles per hour. Antarctica is surrounded by seas and buried under a permanent ice cap three miles thick in places. These ice caps contain 90 percent of the world's ice (70 percent of it is fresh water).

The ocean around Antarctica teems with life, especially during the short summer. Phytoplankton (tiny plant plankton) float near the surface and provide food for zooplankton, which feed crab, fish, and squid. These are eaten by seals, penguins, killer whales, and leopard seals. Krill is also an important food for baleen whales, like the humpback whale. Many seals and seabirds take up temporary residence on land in the summer to molt and breed.

Wandering albatross
With a 10-foot wingspan, the wandering albatross is a powerful flier. It masters southern ocean storms, soaring hundreds of miles in search of squid.

Adélie penguin
To leave the water, Adélie penguins swim to shore and leap up to 10 feet to land on the ice on their feet or stomach. Using their feet and flippers, they toboggan over the ice.

Emperor penguin
Emperor penguins **breed** on the winter ice surrounding Antarctica. The female lays a single egg, which the male keeps warm while he balances on his feet for about 60 days while the female goes to get food.

Humpback whale
The humpback whale feeds in the summer months on krill in the cold Antarctic waters. In the fall, the whales move to warmer waters and do not eat for up to eight months.

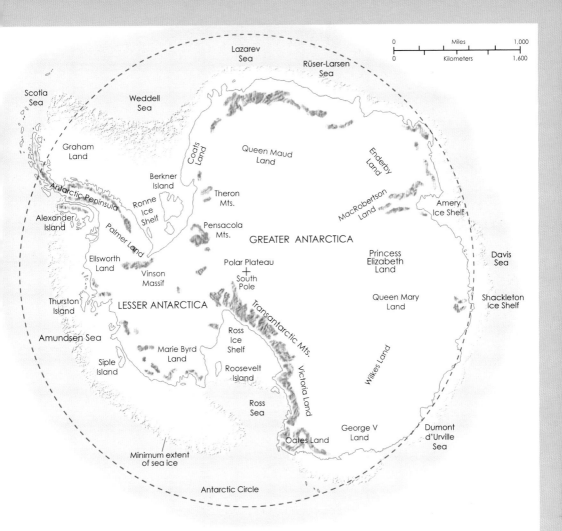

0 ——— Miles ——— 1,000
0 ——— Kilometers ——— 1,600

Lazarev Sea

Rüser-Larsen Sea

Scotia Sea

Weddell Sea

Graham Land

Coats Land

Queen Maud Land

Enderby Land

Antarctic Peninsula

Berkner Island

Theron Mts.

MacRobertson Land

Amery Ice Shelf

Alexander Island

Ronne Ice Shelf

Pensacola Mts.

GREATER ANTARCTICA

Davis Sea

Palmer Land

Ellsworth Land

Polar Plateau

Princess Elizabeth Land

Vinson Massif

+ South Pole

Thurston Island

LESSER ANTARCTICA

Queen Mary Land

Shackleton Ice Shelf

Amundsen Sea

Ross Ice Shelf

Transantarctic Mts.

Marie Byrd Land

Siple Island

Roosevelt Island

Victoria Land

Wilkes Land

Ross Sea

George V Land

Dumont d'Urville Sea

Oates Land

Minimum extent of sea ice

Antarctic Circle

Krill

Krill are finger-length, shrimplike creatures. They provide food for many other animals, such as the blue whale, which eats up to 8,800 pounds of krill per day. Krill breed quickly in these nutrient-rich waters. One female can lay 3,000 eggs in a year.

Elephant seal

The largest seal in the world, the male southern elephant seal, can weigh up to 8,800 pounds. Elephant seals feed on fish and squid and can dive as deep as 5,000 feet.

Leopard seal

A ferocious hunter and a fast swimmer, the leopard seal eats penguins, fish, krill, seals, and their pups. They spend most of their time in the freezing waters and have a thick layer of blubber that keeps them warm.

THE ARCTIC

The Arctic surrounds the North Pole and includes the far north of North America, Asia, Europe, and much of Greenland. However, most of the Arctic is a massive sheet of ice floating on the Arctic Ocean. Conditions here are among the harshest on earth. In midwinter, it is dark 24 hours a day, the temperature drops to –58°F, and freezing winds blast the barren landscape.

Despite this, many animals live here. Polar bears and Arctic foxes are active all year, hunting on the large, moving ice floes. Arctic hares and lemmings burrow in the snow to escape the winter weather. Other animals migrate. The ice sheet shrinks as temperatures rise. Snow melts to reveal the tundra (land where trees cannot grow), and the lower soil is always frozen. But hardy flowers grow and attract insects, which bring out herbivores, such as reindeer, and predators, like wolves.

Polar bear
The polar bear is a powerful swimmer that hunts on the ice floes. Stalking its prey on the ice, it is camouflaged by its coat, and the hairy soles of its feet keep it from slipping.

Arctic fox
The fur of the Arctic fox is gray or brown in the summer, but turns white in the winter to match its surroundings, so it can hunt and **scavenge** without being seen.

Snow goose
Snow geese are not always white—they can be blue or gray. They fly north each spring to breed in the short Arctic summer, where they have virtually no predators or competitors. Snow geese pair for life and raise their young together.

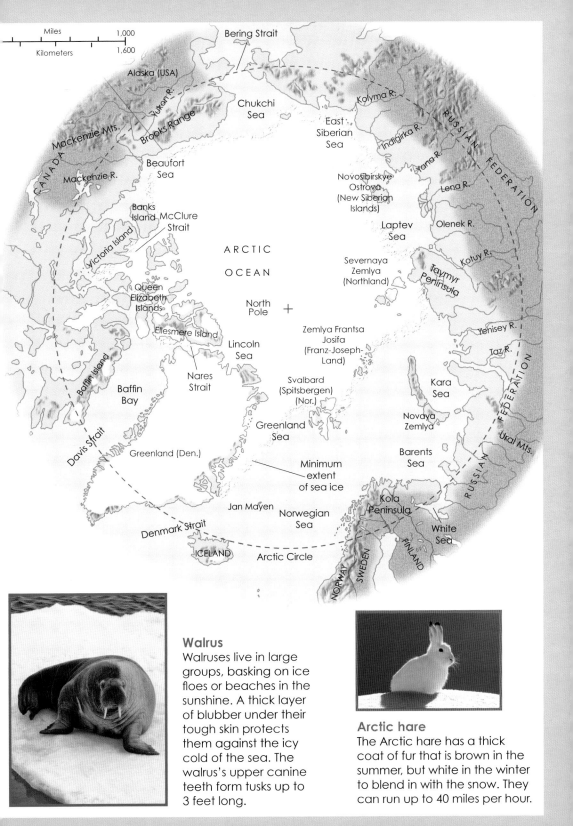

Miles
1,000
Kilometers
1,600

Bering Strait

Alaska (USA)

Chukchi
Sea

Kolyma R.

East
Siberian
Sea

Yukon R.

Brooks Range

RUSSIAN

FEDERATION

Mackenzie Mts.

CANADA

Indigirka R.

Yana R.

Lena R.

Beaufort
Sea

Mackenzie R.

Novosibirskye
Ostrova
(New Siberian
Islands)

Banks
Island
McClure
Strait

Victoria Island

Laptev
Sea

Olenek R.

Kotuy R.

ARCTIC

OCEAN

Severnaya
Zemlya
(Northland)

Taymyr
Peninsula

Queen
Elizabeth
Islands

North
Pole +

Yenisey R.

Ellesmere Island

Lincoln
Sea

Zemlya Frantsa
Josifa
(Franz-Joseph-
Land)

Taz R.

Baffin Island

Nares
Strait

Svalbard
(Spitsbergen)
(Nor.)

Kara
Sea

RUSSIAN

FEDERATION

Baffin
Bay

Novaya
Zemlya

Ural Mts.

Davis Strait

Greenland
Sea

Greenland (Den.)

Minimum
extent
of sea ice

Barents
Sea

Jan Mayen

Norwegian
Sea

Kola
Peninsula

White
Sea

Denmark Strait

RUSSIAN

ICELAND

Arctic Circle

NORWAY

SWEDEN

FINLAND

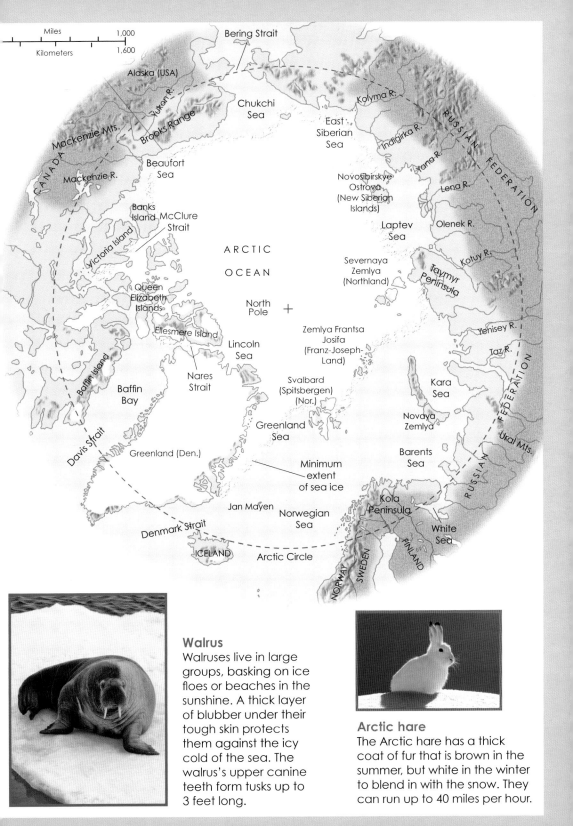

Walrus
Walruses live in large groups, basking on ice floes or beaches in the sunshine. A thick layer of blubber under their tough skin protects them against the icy cold of the sea. The walrus's upper canine teeth form tusks up to 3 feet long.

Arctic hare
The Arctic hare has a thick coat of fur that is brown in the summer, but white in the winter to blend in with the snow. They can run up to 40 miles per hour.

GLOSSARY

Agriculture: The work of growing crops or raising farm animals.

Algae: A simple plant that doesn't have stems, roots, or leaves.

Altitude: How high (or low) something is, as compared to the level of the ocean.

Breed: To give birth or have babies.

Burrow: A hole or tunnel dug by a small animal, such as a rabbit, which is used as its home.

Coniferous: A bush or tree that stays green all year round, such as fir, pine, and spruce trees.

Conservation: The care and protection of forests, wildlife, and natural resources.

Deciduous: A bush or tree that loses its leaves every year, such as maple, birch, and oak trees.

Diversity: Having a great deal of variety. A region that has great diversity of animals is a place that is home to many different kinds of animals.

Drought: A long period of time without rainfall, which leads to a shortage of drinking water for plants and animals in that environment.

Evaporate: When the sun heats up the water in puddles, rivers, lakes, or oceans and turns it into vapor, or steam.

Extinct: No longer existing, or having no living members.

Forage: To search for food.

Habitat: The place where an animal or plant is normally found.

Hibernate: To spend the winter months in a kind of sleep. Some animals and plants hibernate when the temperatures are cold and food is scarce, to help them survive.

Humid: Full of water vapor. The more humid an environment is, the more likely it is to have rain, dew, and fog.

Marshland: Low-lying land that is wet and soft.

Marsupial: A subgroup of mammals that live primarily in Australasia and carry their young in a pouch.

Membrane: A very thin layer of tissue or skin that covers a part of an animal or plant.

Migrate: To move from one region to another, especially when the season changes. Many birds will fly south in wintertime, migrating to a habitat that is warmer.

Omnivore: An animal that eats food from both plant and animal food groups.

Organ: A part of the body that does a particular job.

Pesticide: A chemical used to destroy insects or other pests that are harmful to plants or animals.

Plankton: Tiny plants and animals that drift or float in oceans and lakes.

Polar: Describes something related to the North or South Pole, usually in reference to their cold, icy environment.

Scavenge: To search and gather food that has been left behind.

Scrub: An area of land with small bushes and trees that has wet, mild winters and long, dry summers.

Steppe: A large, flat area with grass but very few trees, common in eastern Europe and Asia.

Taiga: Cold woodland forest areas located in the northern parts of the world.

Talon: A sharp claw of an animal, especially a bird of prey, such as a buzzard, eagle, falcon, hawk, or owl.

THE ANIMALS

Here are some fascinating facts about some of the world's most wonderful animals!

South America

Andean bear—the only bear native to South America

Poison dart frog—one of the most poisonous animals on earth

Capybara—the world's largest rodent

Andean flicker—this bird uses its long tongue to catch ants under bark

Pudu—the smallest deer in the world

Mountain viscacha—a rodent that is as big as a rabbit

Hummingbird—can hover in midair

Vicuna—the smallest member of the camel family

Andean condor—the world's largest bird of prey

Cougar—can leap 20 feet up into a tree

Macaw—has jaws strong enough to crack a Brazil nut

Piranha—has razor-sharp teeth

Sloth—can turn its head 270 degrees

Jaguar—an excellent swimmer

Harpy eagle—the largest and most powerful eagle in the world

North America

Virginia possum—North America's only marsupial

Gallinule—can walk from lily pad to lily pad searching for fish

Everglade kite—this bird's nickname is the "snail kite" because it eats snails

American alligator—can live up to 50 years in the wild

Roadrunner—can run at speeds of up to 19 miles per hour

Desert tortoise—escapes the desert heat by burrowing into the ground

Rattlesnake—there are 16 different types of rattlesnakes

Prairie dog—is not a dog but a type of squirrel

Coyote—is related to the wolf

Skunk—will hiss a warning before it sprays

Armadillo—rolls itself into a ball for protection when threatened

Screech owl—gets its name from its wailing call

Porcupine—has thousands of quills on its back for protection

Moose—can be up to 7½ feet tall

Jackrabbit—babies can run immediately after they are born

Asia

Polecat—a very good climber, but hunts on the ground

Flying lemur—glides from tree to tree as if it is flying

Langur—also known as a "leaf monkey" because it eats leaves

Snow leopard—lives high in the Himalayan mountains

Markhor—its corkscrew horns can grow to 4 feet long

Yak—its long, shaggy coat protects it from the cold

Giant panda—eats bamboo for 16 hours a day

Golden pheasant—builds its nest on the ground in the forests of central China

Suslik—lives in a colony under the ground

Pine marten—uses its sharp claws and tail to climb trees

Onager—can survive in the desert without drinking for up to three days

Mongolian gerbil—stays in its burrow during the day and is active at sunset

Baikal seal—lives in the oldest and deepest lake in Russia

Tiger—the largest member of the cat family

Hill mynah—often mimics the sounds and songs of other birds

Africa

Meerkat—lives in large groups that work together

Impala—can leap up to 33 feet in one bound

Silverback gorilla—the world's largest ape

Nile crocodile—preys on wildebeest, gazelle, and lions

Ostrich—the world's largest bird; it cannot fly

African hunting dog—this social animal lives and hunts in packs

Wildebeest—herds often join together with herds of zebra for protection

Secretary bird—its wings span 6½ feet

Lion—rests up to 20 hours per day

African elephant—a calf can weigh up to 250 pounds at birth

Zebra—its skin is black underneath its hair

Rhino—although it can weigh up to two tons, it can run very fast

Jerboa—this small rodent can hop like a kangaroo

Addax—never needs to drink; gets all of its moisture from grasses and leaves

Dromedary camel—can survive for a week or more without food or water

Australasia

Brain coral—looks like the human brain

Clownfish—hides among anemone for protection

Giant clam—a mollusk that weighs up to 880 pounds

Tiger shark—may have as many as 30,000 teeth in its lifetime

Blue-streaked wrasse—this tiny fish removes parasites from other fish

Brown falcon—one of the most common birds of prey in Australia

Kangaroo—can jump as high as three times its height

Cuscus—a tree-living marsupial

Koala—sleeps more than 20 hours a day

Platypus—the only mammal that lays eggs

Antarctica

Emperor penguin—the male keeps eggs warm until they are ready to hatch

Adélie penguin—can leap 10 feet into the air to exit the water

Leopard seal—has thick blubber to stay warm in freezing water

Killer whale—also called an orca, this is the largest member of the dolphin family

Elephant seal—the largest seal in the world, it can weigh up to 8,800 pounds

Europe

European wildcat—the wild ancestor of the house cat

Brown bear—despite its large size, it can run very fast

Eurasian otter—can close its ears and nostrils when underwater

Eurasian jay—buries food in the fall and finds it in the spring

Eurasian badger—has very poor eyesight

European mole—lives underground in a system of tunnels

Sparrowhawk—the female is larger than the male

European hedgehog—protects itself with sharp spines or by rolling into a ball

Water shrew—eats and sleeps throughout the day and night

Kingfisher—catches fish and then hits them on a branch before eating them

The Arctic

Polar bear—a powerful swimmer, it spends much of its time in the sea.

Snow goose—they pair for life

Arctic fox—the color of its fur changes to match the season

Walrus—its tusks can grow as long as 3 feet

Arctic hare—can hop at speeds of up to 40 miles per hour

DIORAMA ASSEMBLY INSTRUCTIONS

Carefully separate the scenes.

Fold each landscape as indicated in the photographs on the next page.

Match each diorama to its corresponding animal(s).

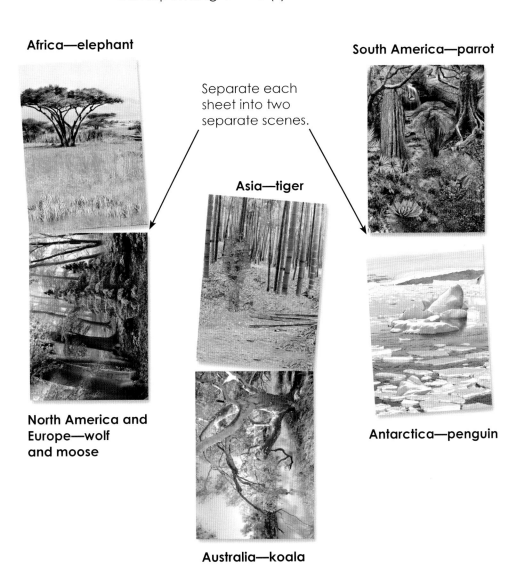

Africa—elephant

Separate each sheet into two separate scenes.

South America—parrot

Asia—tiger

North America and Europe—wolf and moose

Antarctica—penguin

Australia—koala

DIORAMA ASSEMBLY INSTRUCTIONS

North America and Europe

pop out

fold in
flap to
stand

fold
scene
in half

fold in
flap to
stand

Africa

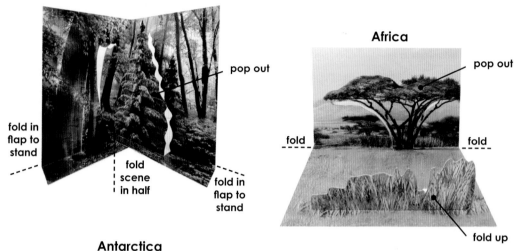

pop out

fold

fold

fold up

Antarctica

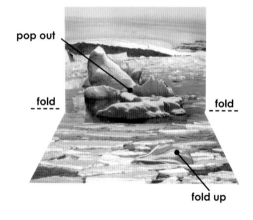

pop out

fold

fold

fold up

Asia

scene
splits here

pop
out

fold

fold

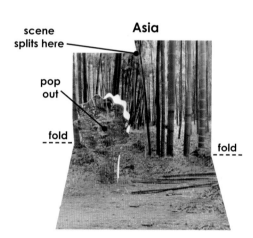

Australia

pop out

fold

fold

South America

pop out

fold

fold

fold up

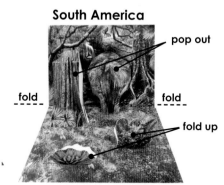